THE POETRY OF SILVER

The Poetry of Silver

Walter the Educator

SKB

Silent King Books a WhichHead imprint

Copyright © 2023 by Walter the Educator

All rights reserved. No part of this book may be reproduced in any manner whatsoever without written permission except in the case of brief quotations embodied in critical articles and reviews.

First Printing, 2023

Disclaimer
This book is a literary work; poems are not about specific persons, locations, situations, and/or circumstances unless mentioned in a historical context. This book is for entertainment and informational purposes only. The author and publisher offer this information without warranties expressed or implied. No matter the grounds, neither the author nor the publisher will be accountable for any losses, injuries, or other damages caused by the reader's use of this book. The use of this book acknowledges an understanding and acceptance of this disclaimer.

"Earning a degree in chemistry changed my life!"
- Walter the Educator

dedicated to all the chemistry lovers, like myself, across the world

CONTENTS

Dedication V

Why I Created This Book? 1

One - Treasure To Behold 2

Two - Shall Reside 4

Three - Forever To Last 6

Four - Eternal Throne 8

Five - Silver's Allure 10

Six - Revered By All 12

Seven - Guardian Of Hearts 14

Eight - Precious Sight 16

Nine - Conductor Of Dreams 18

Ten - Sweet Release 20

Eleven - Cherish This Metal 22

Twelve - Shimmering Light 24

Thirteen - Metal Divine 26

Fourteen - Symphony Of Dreams 28

Fifteen - Silver, The Element 30

Sixteen - Timeless Treasure 32

Seventeen - Ancient Reveries 34

Eighteen - Silver's Legacy 36

Nineteen - Jewel Of The Earth 38

Twenty - Dreams Come Alive 40

Twenty-One - Space And Time 42

Twenty-Two - Through And Through 44

Twenty-Three - Fragile Dance 46

Twenty-Four - Joy And The Pain 48

Twenty-Five - Love's Tender Escapade . . . 50

Twenty-Six - Memories Never Fade 52

Twenty-Seven - Secrets It Keeps 54

Twenty-Eight - Free Of Stain 56

Twenty-Nine - Precious And Rare 58

Thirty - Silver, Precious Silver 60

Thirty-One - Masterpiece Of Art 62

Thirty-Two - Enduring Worth 64

Thirty-Three - Precious Prize	66
Thirty-Four - Passion Within	68
Thirty-Five - Celestial Light	70
About The Author	72

WHY I CREATED THIS BOOK?

Creating a book about the chemical element of silver can serve several purposes. Firstly, silver is a fascinating element with a rich history and numerous applications. Exploring its properties, uses, and significance can provide valuable insights into the world of chemistry and materials science. Moreover, a book about silver can delve into its cultural, economic, and societal significance throughout history. From its use as currency and jewelry to its role in photography and technology, silver has had a profound impact on human civilization. This book can also educate readers about the environmental and health aspects of silver. Overall, this book about silver can enlighten readers about the science, history, and practical applications of this versatile element, making it an engaging and informative resource for both experts and enthusiasts alike.

ONE

TREASURE TO BEHOLD

In forests deep, where secrets lie,
A metal gleams beneath the sky.
Silver, precious and divine,
A treasure sought by hearts entwined.

Born of stars and cosmic might,
In the depths of a stellar flight.
Mined from Earth's enduring crust,
A gem concealed, a hidden trust.

Silver, radiant as the moon's glow,
Whispers secrets only few may know.
Its lustrous sheen, a dazzling sight,
Reflecting dreams in the darkest night.

A conductor of energy and light,
A catalyst in nature's fight.

Silver's touch, a healing grace,
A balm to wounds we can't erase.
    Adorned on wrists, in rings of love,
A symbol of grace from high above.
Silver, noble and steadfast,
A reminder of moments that forever last.
    In tales of old, legends unfold,
Of silver's worth, more than its weight in gold.
A currency of ancient lore,
A testament to the stories it bore.
    Silver, silent guardian of time,
Eternal beauty in its prime.
From alchemy's touch to modern days,
Its legacy forever stays.
    So, cherish the gleam that silver imparts,
A precious metal that captures hearts.
In its essence, a beauty untold,
Silver, a treasure to behold.

TWO

SHALL RESIDE

In the realm of gleaming light, a precious metal dwells,
Born of stars and forged with grace, a beauty that excels.
Silver, radiant and pure, adorns the Earth's enduring crust,
A gift from ancient depths, in treasures we entrust.

    With argent sheen, it dances, reflecting cosmic rays,
Conducting energy and light through its magnificent haze.
A conduit of power, it hums with electric might,
Unleashing its potential, a symphony of cosmic light.

    Silver, the healer's touch, a balm for body and soul,
Its mystical properties, ancient secrets to unfold.
In wounds it soothes, in ailments it brings relief,
A guardian of wellness, a source of boundless belief.

Symbol of love's devotion, a token of affection's worth,
Silver whispers promises, a bond that spans the Earth.
Through ages it has shimmered, a currency of trust,
A precious metal's value, in silver we entrust.

Time's faithful guardian, a mirror to the past,
Silver echoes history, memories that forever last.
From ancient civilizations to modern realms we see,
Silver's enduring legacy, a tale of destiny.

Cherish the beauty, treasure this divine alloy,
Silver, a gift from cosmos, a source of endless joy.
Embrace its radiant glow, let its essence be your guide,
For in the realm of silver, true beauty shall reside.

THREE

FOREVER TO LAST

In the realm of mystic alchemy,
There exists a metal of purity,
Born of stars and Earth's own crust,
A treasure divine, forever just.

Silver, the enchanting light it holds,
A lustrous sheen that never folds,
Reflecting beams in radiant gleam,
A shimmering dance, a silver dream.

Conductor of energy, conductor of light,
Silver's touch, a celestial sight,
Transmitting power with ethereal grace,
A conduit for energy's embrace.

A healer's touch, gentle and true,
Silver's essence, a potent brew,
Curative powers, ancient and old,
Reviving spirits, mending the soul.

Symbol of love, a token adored,
Silver's presence, forever restored,
In rings and bands, a union sealed,
Two hearts entwined, a love revealed.

Through time and space, silver has reigned,
A currency, a trade, a wealth sustained,
From ancient civilizations to modern age,
Silver's worth, an enduring stage.

Cherish the beauty, embrace its gleam,
Silver, a marvel, a precious dream,
A guardian of wellness, a mirror to the past,
Silver's essence, forever to last.

FOUR

ETERNAL THRONE

In the realm of shimmering light,
Silver gleams, a celestial sight.
Born of stars, with cosmic might,
A precious metal, pure and bright.

    Lustrous sheen, captivating grace,
Silver's allure, no one can erase.
Conductor of energy, it takes its place,
Guiding currents with elegant embrace.

    A guardian of time, a keeper of lore,
Silver whispers tales of days of yore.
A currency of trust, forevermore,
Symbolizing love, devotion it bore.

    Healing touch, a soothing balm,
Silver mends, with a gentle calm.

A token of affection, a lover's psalm,
Embracing souls, in a seraphic realm.
    Across time and space, its presence known,
Silver's worth, an eternal throne.
Cherish its beauty, let its gleam be shown,
For silver's enchantment, forever grown.

FIVE

SILVER'S ALLURE

In the depths of Earth's ancient crust,
A gem of silver lies concealed,
Its gleam, a treasure yet untold,
A story waiting to be revealed.
  A conductor of energy and light,
Silver dances with electric might,
Unleashing sparks that illuminate,
The darkness in the dead of night.
  Symbol of grace, symbol of love,
Silver threads that bind hearts above,
It weaves a tapestry of dreams,
A shimmering moonbeam, so it seems.
  Reflecting cosmic rays from the sky,
Silver whispers secrets, oh, so sly,

Healing wounds with its tender touch,
A soothing balm, it means so much.

A symbol of trust, a symbol of history,
Silver stands as a guardian of mystery,
A precious metal, rare and pure,
In its embrace, we find strength secure.

Enchanting light, a radiant glow,
Silver's essence, it loves to show,
Conductor of energy, it takes its flight,
Guiding us through the darkest night.

Cherish the beauty, embrace the gleam,
Silver's allure, like a timeless dream,
For in its depths, we find solace and grace,
A precious gift, in this mortal race.

SIX

REVERED BY ALL

In silver's gleam, a healing touch,
A precious metal that means so much.
Its shimmering light, like moonlit skies,
Reflects the beauty that never dies.

Silver, a symbol of purity and grace,
A metal that time cannot erase.
With its lustrous glow, it captures the eye,
A gentle reminder, as days go by.

A silver spoon, a healing balm,
Soothing wounds with its calming calm.
It mends the broken, eases the pain,
A precious gift, like a gentle rain.

Silver threads woven through the night,
Guiding souls towards love's pure light.
It dances with stars, a cosmic embrace,
Transcending boundaries of time and space.

Silent conductor of energy and might,
Silver weaves dreams in the darkest night.
It carries the whispers of secrets untold,
Unveiling mysteries, yet to unfold.

Silver, a treasure from ancient lands,
A testament to skilled craftsman's hands.
From jewelry to coins, its worth is known,
A symbol of value, forever shown.

In the realm of elements, silver stands tall,
A precious metal, revered by all.
Its magic and charm will forever shine,
A timeless beauty, eternally divine.

SEVEN

GUARDIAN OF HEARTS

In the realm of healing, a shimmering delight,
Silver emerges, a guardian of light.
Its touch, so gentle, it mends the soul,
A remedy for wounds, making hearts whole.

A precious metal, with powers untold,
Silver's allure, like moonlit gold.
Symbol of purity, a mirror to reflect,
The depth of emotions, the love we protect.

Silver, the essence of time's embrace,
Eternity's whispers, it holds in its grace.
A conductor of memories, a vessel of dreams,
Silver, the keeper of life's eternal streams.

In its radiant glow, joy finds its way,
A symphony of laughter, a sunlit display.

Sparkling like stars, in the night's embrace,
Silver dances, adorned with grace.
    Oh, silver, the alchemist's dream,
A potion of healing, a celestial gleam.
From ancient realms to modern lore,
Silver's magic forevermore.
    A guardian of hearts, a source of light,
Silver, the element that ignites.
In its embrace, we find solace and peace,
A timeless beauty that will never cease.

EIGHT

PRECIOUS SIGHT

    Silver, a gleaming gift from the earth,
A metal of infinite worth.
Within its essence, secrets unfold,
A story of love, trust, and bold.

    A healer, it whispers with gentle grace,
Soothing wounds, leaving no trace.
Its touch, a balm for the weary soul,
Restoring what once was broken and whole.

    In the moon's soft glow, it dances and gleams,
Reflecting dreams and eternal streams.
Symbolizing purity, love's divine art,
A treasure that captivates every heart.

    Through the ages, it has stood the test,
A symbol of value, forever blessed.
From ancient civilizations to modern day,
Silver's allure never fades away.

    A conductor of energy, it guides and heals,
A bridge between worlds, unlocking zeal.
In its shimmering glow, dreams take flight,
Igniting hope in the darkest night.
    Oh, silver, you are a precious sight,
A beacon of beauty, sparkling so bright.
In your essence, a magic resides,
Eternal and enchanting, forever our guide.

NINE

CONDUCTOR OF DREAMS

In the realm of energies, there lies a silver glow,
A conductor of power, a mystical show.
Silver, the element, pure and bright,
Weaving its tales in the shroud of night.

A symbol of trust, throughout history's reign,
A metal adorned by the noble and plain.
From ancient civilizations to modern day,
Silver's allure never fades away.

It heals the wounds, a balm divine,
With touch as gentle as moonlit shine.
Its essence, a soothing embrace,
Mending hearts with its radiant grace.

Now let us delve into another realm,
Where silver's secrets take the helm.

A guardian of mystery, it holds the key,
Unlocking dreams, setting spirits free.
    A precious gift, bestowed on few,
A conductor of dreams, both old and new.
It dances in moonbeams, whispers in the breeze,
Guiding souls through ethereal seas.
    Oh, silver, you hold time within your grasp,
A reflection of memories, both present and past.
With every touch, a story unfolds,
Of love, of loss, of legends untold.
    A symbol of purity, shining so bright,
A treasure of value, a precious light.
Silver, the element that captures the soul,
In its timeless allure, we forever behold.

TEN

SWEET RELEASE

In the realm of elements, silver shines bright,
A conductor of energy, a guardian of light.
Its lustrous hue, a celestial dance,
A symbol of trust, healing, and chance.

Silver, the whisperer of cosmic tales,
A prism of wonder, where mystery prevails.
It weaves its enchantment, a spell so grand,
Guiding us through the realms, hand in hand.

A guardian of time, it captures the past,
Reflecting the memories that forever last.
In its gleaming surface, secrets reside,
A tapestry of history, never to hide.

From ancient civilizations to modern days,
Silver's touch, an eternal blaze.
Its silvery song, a symphony of grace,
A testament to its everlasting embrace.

    Through the ages, it has stood strong,
A beacon of hope, where hearts belong.
Silver, a companion in life's great quest,
A testament to beauty, a treasure at best.
    So let us cherish this sacred metal of old,
A gift from the heavens, a story untold.
For in its presence, we find solace and peace,
Silver, a testament to love's sweet release.

ELEVEN

CHERISH THIS METAL

Silver, the conductor of energy's flow,
A metal that gleams with a gentle glow.
Symbol of value, a treasure untold,
A guardian of mystery, a story unfold.

In the hands of artisans, it takes its form,
Crafted with care, a beauty to adorn.
From jewelry to coins, its worth is known,
A precious metal, a value it has shown.

But silver is more than mere material,
It's a gift bestowed, ethereal and surreal.
A keeper of memories, a vessel of time,
Reflecting the moments, both yours and mine.

Like moonlight on water, it casts a soft beam,
A source of light, a dreamer's gleam.
It dances with shadows, brings brilliance to sight,
An enchanting presence in the darkest of night.

Silver, a symbol of purity's grace,
A mirror of life's journey, a delicate embrace.
It holds the past, unlocks secrets untold,
A timeless allure, a story to unfold.

Cherish this metal, this companion so dear,
For in its presence, love's release draws near.
Silver, a testament to life's fleeting bliss,
A constant reminder of the memories we miss.

TWELVE

SHIMMERING LIGHT

In the realm of dreams, where shadows dance,
There lies a metal of purest chance.
Silver, the conductor of energy untold,
Unveils the secrets that the night does hold.

A shimmering tapestry, woven with grace,
In moonlight's embrace, it finds its place.
The whispers of secrets, it carries with pride,
Through realms of darkness, where they reside.

Silver, the alchemist of visions unseen,
A bridge between worlds, where dreams convene.
It captures the essence of hopes and desires,
Igniting a spark that sets souls on fire.

Its gleaming surface, a reflection of time,
Mirroring memories, both yours and mine.

A symbol of purity, in its radiant glow,
A testament to love's sweet release, it shows.
   Cherish this metal, this gift from above,
A guardian of hearts, a beacon of love.
For silver is more than mere metal and ore,
It's the key to unlock dreams and explore.
   So let it guide you, with its shimmering light,
Through the darkest of nights, towards love's pure sight.
Silver, the precious sight that we adore,
A guardian of mystery, forevermore.

THIRTEEN

METAL DIVINE

In the realm of dreams, where shadows dance,
There lies a metal, a gleaming chance.
Silver, the conductor of ethereal schemes,
Weaver of enchantment, guardian of dreams.

    Its lustrous glow, a moonlit embrace,
Reflects the mysteries of time and space.
A touch of silver, a whisper of grace,
Unveiling secrets, a glimpse of embrace.

    Through the looking glass, memories unfold,
Silver's reflection, a story untold.
Moments captured, frozen in time,
A silver mirror, an eternal rhyme.

    Oh, silver, timeless allure,
A shimmering path, pure and sure.

A symbol of purity, a gleaming light,
Guiding us through the darkest night.
    Keeper of time, a silent vow,
Silver's touch, eternal now.
A key to the realms, the gateways unseen,
Unlocking dreams, exploring new scenes.
    So let us cherish this metal divine,
Silver, the element, forever entwined.
In its embrace, we find solace and grace,
A shining reminder, of dreams we chase.

FOURTEEN

SYMPHONY OF DREAMS

In the realm of dreams, where shadows dance,
There lies a guardian in a silver trance.
A shimmering hue, a lustrous gleam,
Silver, the element of endless esteem.

A vessel of time, a conduit of grace,
Silver weaves tales in its ethereal space.
A reflection of memories, both old and new,
It whispers of secrets that only it knew.

A symbol of purity, untouched and pristine,
Silver enchants with its radiant sheen.
It adorns the world with a heavenly glow,
A reminder of love and moments we sow.

With every touch, it leaves an imprint,
A mark of affection, forever imprinted.

It captures the essence of cherished days,
And in its embrace, memories forever stay.

    Oh, silver, the timeless allure you possess,
Unlocking dreams in your gentle caress.
Exploring new scenes, in your light we see,
A precious gift, forever treasured, you'll be.

    So let us celebrate this element divine,
With silver's embrace, our hearts intertwine.
For in its mystique, a magic lies,
A symphony of dreams, soaring the skies.

FIFTEEN

SILVER, THE ELEMENT

In the realm of shadows, a guardian stands,
A silvery sentinel, with secrets in its hands.
Silver, the conductor of dreams untold,
A metal of mystique, a wonder to behold.

Its surface gleams, a mirror of the night,
Reflecting the stars, shimmering with light.
A symbol of purity, untarnished and bright,
Silver's radiance casts away the blight.

Through the annals of time, it has endured,
A timeless allure, forever assured.
In its depths lie memories, steadfast and true,
Whispering tales of a world we once knew.

Silver, the vessel that carries our past,
A mirror of moments, a treasure that lasts.

Its gentle glow, a beacon of grace,
Guiding us through life's intricate maze.
    A source of light, in darkness it shines,
A guardian of hearts, a love that defines.
Silver, a key to unlock dreams untold,
Unveiling new realms, a beauty to behold.
    So let us cherish this metal divine,
A gift from the cosmos, a treasure so fine.
Silver, the element that captures our gaze,
In its radiant sheen, our wonder it plays.

SIXTEEN

TIMELESS TREASURE

Silver, oh vessel of time,
A metal that glistens and chimes.
A symbol of purity and grace,
Reflecting light in every space.
    Guardian of hearts, so true,
Unlocking dreams, it knows what to do.
With a touch, it ignites a spark,
Guiding souls through the dark.
    Silver, a mirror of memories,
Capturing moments, like ancient reveries.
Each tarnish, a story etched in grace,
A reminder of love's enduring embrace.
    Its allure, a radiance so rare,
A shimmering beauty beyond compare.

In its presence, hearts are held,
In its shine, dreams are compelled.
    Enduring as a timeless treasure,
Silver's worth knows no measure.
From ancient civilizations to modern days,
Its value forever stays.
    So let us cherish this precious metal,
A gem that shines in every petal.
For silver, in all its gleaming array,
Is a gift that never fades away.

SEVENTEEN

ANCIENT REVERIES

In the realm of metal, a vessel of time,
Silver gleams, a radiant chime.
A source of light, ethereal and pure,
Shimmering in darkness, a luminescent allure.
    Silver, a reflection of hopes and desires,
Guardian of hearts, igniting fires.
Unlocking dreams, with its shimmering key,
Revealing paths, where souls long to be.
    A keeper of memories, through ages past,
Guiding us through darkness, casting shadows vast.
A mark of affection, in tokens of love,
Silver's embrace, like whispers from above.
    Its allure enduring, a timeless embrace,
Capturing the essence of cherished days.

A vessel for our past, preserved in its sheen,
A gift of silver, a treasure evergreen.
    Now, let us unveil a new tale to be told,
Of silver's grace, a beacon bold.
Guardian of hearts, it lights the way,
Leading souls through the dark, come what may.
    A mirror of memories, ancient reveries,
Capturing moments like whispered mysteries.
Enduring worth, a gift that won't fade,
Silver's legacy, an eternal serenade.

EIGHTEEN

SILVER'S LEGACY

In the depths of darkness, a guiding light,
Silver emerges, shimmering so bright.
A lustrous metal, with elegance untold,
Its radiance captivating, a story to unfold.

    A mark of affection, a symbol of grace,
Silver's embrace, like a warm embrace.
It adorns our fingers, our necks, and our wrists,
A testament to love, forever persist.

    A vessel for cherished memories, it holds,
A touch of silver, a tale unfolds.
From ancient times to the present day,
Silver's allure, it never fades away.

    Through history's pages, it weaves a thread,
Moments captured, dreams unlocked and spread.

From coins to jewelry, its value is renowned,
Silver's legacy, forever profound.
   Radiant and pure, a guardian of hearts,
Silver's enchantment, it never departs.
It shields and protects, a precious embrace,
A love that endures, a timeless space.
   A mirror of memories, reflecting the past,
Silver's reflection, forever to last.
In its gleaming surface, stories reside,
Of lives well-lived, of journeys worldwide.
   Oh, silver, majestic and fine,
Your essence, a treasure so divine.
With every glimmer, a story is told,
In silver's presence, we find pure gold.

NINETEEN

JEWEL OF THE EARTH

In the realm of dreams, a shimmering light,
Silver emerges, gleaming so bright.
A vessel for memories, precious and rare,
Silent guardian of hearts, forever to care.
   With every touch, a tale unfolds,
Of love that endures, as time unfolds.
A symbol of connection, bound by trust,
Silver, the metal, turns dreams into dust.
   It captures the essence of cherished days,
Guiding us through darkness, in mysterious ways.
Reflecting the moon, its ethereal gleam,
Silver whispers secrets, like a forgotten dream.
   Oh, silver, you hold the power to unlock,
The depths of our hearts, the dreams that we've blocked.

A mirror of emotions, both pure and true,
In your delicate embrace, we find solace anew.
   Through the passage of time, your worth remains,
An enduring legacy, that never wanes.
For you are not just a metal, cold and gray,
But a treasure of beauty that will never fade away.
   So let us celebrate, the allure of silver's embrace,
Embracing its magic, with every step we trace.
In its lustrous glow, we find solace and mirth,
Silver, the element, the jewel of the earth.

TWENTY

DREAMS COME ALIVE

Silver, vessel of memories untold,
A shimmering light in the darkness, behold!
Guardian of hearts, protector of dreams,
In your lustrous embrace, love's eternal streams.

Enduring allure, in your gleaming sheen,
Moments captured, forever pristine.
Through ages past, your worth proclaimed,
A precious treasure, history's acclaimed.

Radiant beauty, like moonlight's embrace,
Reflecting the world's enigmatic grace.
You shine with a brilliance that none can compare,
A metallic symphony, a sight so rare.

Mirror of memories, you hold within,
Whispers of stories, where secrets begin.
Unlocking the depths of our very souls,
Revealing the truth, making us whole.

    Silver, oh silver, enchanting and true,
Your silent power, forever we pursue.
In your ethereal presence, dreams come alive,
A testament to the magic you derive.
    So let us cherish this element divine,
Embrace its mystique, let it forever shine.
For silver, dear silver, you are a treasure untold,
A symphony of memories, a love to behold.

TWENTY-ONE

SPACE AND TIME

Silver, a vessel of memories,
A shimmering key to dreams untold.
In its radiant glow, the past unfolds,
A timeless beauty that forever pleases.
    Silver, a source of ethereal light,
Reflecting the moon's purest beams.
Its lustrous gleam, a poet's dreams,
A symphony of brilliance, shining so bright.
    Oh, silver, how you allure us all,
With your elegance and enduring worth.
A precious metal, treasured since birth,
A gift to be cherished, never to fall.
    A guardian of hearts, a mirror of memories,
Silver captures moments, preserves tales.

Its polished surface, a mirror that never fails,
To reflect the love, the joy, the mysteries.
    Embrace the power of silver's gleaming grace,
Unlock the emotions, let them roam free.
In its timeless legacy, we are set free,
To dance with silver, in its eternal embrace.
    So let us celebrate silver's beauty divine,
A precious metal that forever shines.
In its enchanting allure, we find,
A treasure that transcends space and time.

TWENTY-TWO

THROUGH AND THROUGH

In the realm of elements, a treasure so rare,
Silver, the guardian of hearts, beyond compare.
A metal divine, with ethereal sheen,
Unleashing emotions, a sight so serene.

Its essence, a mirror of memories untold,
Reflecting the tales of the young and the old.
A shimmering canvas, where secrets reside,
Unveiling the depths of the soul, far and wide.

Like moonlight's embrace on a tranquil night,
Silver's allure casts a spell, shining bright.
A symphony of echoes, a whispering breeze,
Unraveling the mysteries, as time flees.

A touch of elegance, it bestows upon all,
Unveiling the beauty, in every rise and fall.

A silent companion, through moments of bliss,
An eternal witness, to love's tender kiss.
   Oh, silver, a treasure that outshines the rest,
A legacy of beauty, forever blessed.
Capturing the essence of life's fragile dance,
Preserving the stories, in its timeless expanse.
   So, let us cherish this metal divine,
A glimpse of heaven, in every design.
For silver, the element, so pure and true,
Unveils the world's enigmatic grace, through and through.

TWENTY-THREE

FRAGILE DANCE

In the realm of dreams, where memories fade,
Silver emerges, a guardian of hearts.
Its ethereal glow, a celestial cascade,
Mirrors the past, where time imparts.

A touch of elegance, a shimmering hue,
Silver whispers secrets, lost and found.
It holds the tales that once were true,
A reflection of the world going 'round.

Unlocking emotions, revealing the truth,
Silver dances with shadows of the soul.
Its radiant light, a beacon of youth,
Unveiling the stories that make us whole.

With allure and grace, it captures the night,
Enduring worth, forever in flight.

Moments frozen, forever in sight,
Silver's legacy, a timeless delight.
   Elegance personified, a symphony of echoes,
Silver's voice, a gentle serenade.
A silent companion, it softly bestows,
Witness to love's tender escapade.
   A treasure it is, outshining the rest,
Capturing life's fragile dance.
Silver, the essence of every jest,
Forever gleaming, in eternal trance.

TWENTY-FOUR

JOY AND THE PAIN

In the realm of shadows, where secrets reside,
There gleams a treasure, where dreams coincide.
Silver, the element that captures the night,
Unveiling stories, frozen in its light.

It dances with grace, on a moonlit stage,
A symphony of whispers, an eternal pledge.
Reflecting the stars, in its shimmering hue,
Silver weaves tales, both old and anew.

From ancient civilizations, it holds their lore,
The conquests of empires, forevermore.
It witnessed the rise and fall of kings,
Capturing history in its delicate wings.

But beyond the past, it holds a key,
Unlocking emotions, setting them free.

A silent companion, in love's tender escapade,
Revealing truths, in shadows it's made.

    Silver, the beacon of youth's sweet embrace,
Unveiling moments that time cannot erase.
It captures the laughter, the joy and the pain,
Weaving a tapestry, that forever will remain.

    Oh, precious silver, so elegant and rare,
Your enduring worth, beyond compare.
In your radiant presence, the night comes alive,
Freezing moments in time, where memories thrive.

    So, let us cherish this element divine,
For in its allure, endless stories entwine.
Silver, the guardian of life's fragile dance,
Preserving our tales, in its timeless expanse.

TWENTY-FIVE

LOVE'S TENDER ESCAPADE

In the realm of dreams, where secrets lie,
There dwells a guardian, silent and shy.
Silver, the keeper of emotions untold,
A precious metal that glistens like gold.

With enigmatic grace, it reflects the light,
Unveiling the mysteries of day and night.
A mirror to the soul, it captures the gaze,
Unraveling stories of forgotten days.

Silver, a vessel of memories profound,
In its shimmering depths, treasures are found.
It holds the laughter, the tears, and the pain,
Preserving them softly, like a gentle refrain.

Oh, silver, how you enchant and beguile,
With elegance that transcends every mile.

Your enduring worth, like a timeless heirloom,
Outshines the rest, casting shadows in gloom.
  Like a moonlit dance on a starry night,
You shimmer and shimmer, a mesmerizing sight.
Unlocking emotions, you hold the key,
To hearts that are longing, wild and free.
  So let us embrace you, precious and rare,
And cherish the moments that we both share.
For silver, dear silver, you'll forever be,
A silent companion in love's tender escapade.

TWENTY-SIX

MEMORIES NEVER FADE

Silver, the guardian of memories,
Capturing moments, preserving tales,
A shimmering reflection of life's mysteries,
In its radiant light, the heart prevails.
    Elegance adorns its metallic sheen,
An enduring worth, beyond compare,
A precious treasure, forever serene,
A whispered secret, it's eager to share.
    Oh, silver, your allure is vast,
A beauty that time cannot erase,
Unlocking emotions, holding them fast,
In your tender embrace.
    A dance, fragile and rare,
You guide us through life's intricate maze,

Revealing truths, setting emotions free,
In your silvery, shimmering blaze.

    Silent companion, steadfast and true,
You witness our joys and our despair,
Preserving stories, capturing essence,
With each polished, gleaming layer.

    Beacon of youth, forever aglow,
Guardian of love's tender escapade,
You hold laughter, tears, and pain,
In your embrace, memories never fade.

    Embrace silver, cherish its gleam,
For in its presence, life's wonders are seen.

TWENTY-SEVEN

SECRETS IT KEEPS

In the realm of silence, it gleams,
A companion of whispers, it seems.
Silver, the keeper of stories untold,
In its lustrous embrace, memories unfold.

A glimmering tapestry, woven with grace,
Capturing moments, time cannot erase.
Its ethereal glow, a celestial light,
Guiding us through the darkest of night.

Oh, silver, how you enchant and allure,
A treasure so pure, so elegant, so pure.
With every flicker, a symphony of shine,
A gift from the heavens, so divine.

Unveiling secrets, like an ancient key,
Revealing truths, only the heart can see.
A mirror of emotions, reflections so deep,
Silver, the guardian, our secrets it keeps.

A testament to love, both old and new,
A testament to strength, in all that we do.
In its gentle touch, a promise it beholds,
To cherish, to protect, as our story unfolds.

Embrace its beauty, let its essence imbue,
For silver holds wonders, both old and new.
A silent companion, a guardian of worth,
Let it guide you, in love and in mirth.

TWENTY-EIGHT

FREE OF STAIN

In silver's gleam, a tale unfolds,
A symphony of secrets yet untold.
Its lustrous sheen, a timeless dance,
Reflects the beauty of life's fleeting chance.

From moonlit nights to twinkling stars,
Silver weaves its magic, near and far.
It captures moments, frozen in time,
A silent witness to love's tender rhyme.

With every touch, it whispers a story,
Of passion, longing, and untold glory.
A symbol of grace, it softly gleams,
In the moonlit shadows of lovers' dreams.

Oh, silver, you're a silent companion,
Guarding love's tender escapade, unbroken.
Through joy and tears, you remain,
A steadfast presence, free of stain.

Your worth, enduring, stands the test,
A precious metal, of purity blessed.
In your embrace, emotions unfold,
Unveiling treasures, untold.

So, let us cherish your shimmering light,
And hold you close, through day and night.
For in your essence, we find solace and grace,
Silver, the keeper of life's delicate embrace.

TWENTY-NINE

PRECIOUS AND RARE

In the realm where silence glows,
A companion serene, Silver shows.
Guardian of love's tender escapade,
In its lustrous embrace, secrets are laid.
    A symbol of grace, pure and refined,
Silver's allure, eternally kind.
Unveiling emotions with shimmering light,
Preserving moments, both day and night.
    Oh, cherish this metal, so precious and rare,
For its worth endures, beyond compare.
In its gleam, a story untold,
Of dreams and desires, it gently holds.
    A treasure, entrusted with life's delicate embrace,
Silver's radiance, a celestial grace.

Its touch, like moonbeams on gentle breeze,
Whispering tales of eternal ease.
    Through time's embrace, its beauty unfolds,
A symphony of silver, forever untold.
So let us adorn our lives with its sheen,
And let its presence eternally gleam.
    For silver, the keeper of memories and dreams,
Is more than a metal, or what it seems.
It's a silent companion, forever in sight,
Guiding us through life's darkest night.
    So hold it close, let its light shine bright,
For silver's embrace is a heavenly sight.
In its presence, love's essence is found,
A silver symphony, forever profound.

THIRTY

SILVER, PRECIOUS SILVER

In Silver's gleaming touch, memories unfold,
A radiant presence, enduring worth untold.
Through time's gentle flow, it captures each glance,
Reflecting life's tapestry in a shimmering dance.
   It holds the whispers of love's tender embrace,
Moments of joy, etched in its radiant grace.
With every passing breath, it softly preserves,
Emotions, like treasures, it gently observes.
   Silver, the guardian of secrets untold,
Unlocks the heart's desires, as stories unfold.
Its enchanting aura, a mystical spell,
Unveiling the depths where emotions dwell.
   In its gentle embrace, love's flame is ignited,
A mirror to the soul, where passions are sighted.

It carries the weight of dreams yet to be,
A vessel of hope, where futures are set free.

    Oh, silver, pure and true, in your embrace,
Whispers of memories find a sacred space.
A keeper of moments, a guardian of dreams,
In your radiant glow, eternity gleams.

    Forever you'll remain, a symbol so pure,
Reflecting life's beauty, forever endure.
In your timeless allure, we find solace and peace,
Silver, precious silver, our hearts never cease.

THIRTY-ONE

MASTERPIECE OF ART

In the realm of elements, a treasure gleams,
A luminescent metal that dances in dreams.
Silver, the vessel of hope and desire,
A mirror to the soul, a flame to inspire.

Beneath its surface, secrets reside,
Whispers of love and emotions untied.
A shimmering aura, enchanting and bright,
Unveiling the depths where emotions take flight.

Oh, silver, keeper of moments untold,
Guardian of dreams, a presence so bold.
Reflecting life's beauty, both vibrant and still,
In your presence, solace and peace gently spill.

You carry the weight of dreams, it seems,
Igniting love's flame, fulfilling our schemes.
A symbol of purity, steadfast and true,
In your embrace, love's light shines through.

Silver, you bind us, a thread through our days,
A testament to beauty in myriad ways.
From jewelry to coins, a legacy grand,
You grace our world with a delicate hand.
So, let us cherish your gleaming embrace,
A testament to life's elegance and grace.
Silver, the element that captures the heart,
Forever enchanting, a masterpiece of art.

THIRTY-TWO

ENDURING WORTH

In silver's gleam, a story unfolds,
A tale of secrets, untold.
A guardian of emotions and memories,
A shimmering metal, with endless reveries.

Beneath the moonlight's tender gaze,
Silver dances in a silent haze,
Reflecting dreams in its gentle sheen,
A testament to all that's unseen.

Silver, the alchemy of purity,
A cosmic gift, with enduring worth.
Its radiant glow, a timeless treasure,
A symbol of love, beyond measure.

It whispers softly in the night,
A companion in the darkest hour,
With silent strength and steadfast might,
Silver weaves a tapestry of power.

A vessel for dreams, it holds them dear,
Glimmering hopes, whispering near.
In silver's embrace, dreams take flight,
Guided by its luminous light.

Oh, silver, guardian of dreams,
With elegance and grace, it gleams.
A symbol of beauty, delicate and pure,
In its radiant aura, hearts find a cure.

So let us cherish this precious metal,
A shimmering treasure, never to settle.
For silver's beauty, forever will shine,
A celestial gift, divine and sublime.

THIRTY-THREE

PRECIOUS PRIZE

In silver's gleam, a world of dreams,
Where hopes and wishes softly gleam.
A metal rare, a precious prize,
With powers that unfold surprise.
    Silver, the guardian of dreams,
Reflecting moonlight's gentle beams.
It holds within its shining sheen,
The magic of what could have been.
    A symbol of love, true and pure,
A vessel for dreams to endure.
In its embrace, hearts find solace,
As dreams dance with ethereal grace.
    Oh, silver, with elegance untold,
Your beauty shines, a sight to behold.

From jewelry's touch to silverware,
A touch of grace that's beyond compare.
    A whispered promise, a gentle sigh,
In silver's glow, troubles pass by.
It brings us peace, serenity's embrace,
A respite from life's hectic pace.
    And in the quiet of the night,
Silver guides us with its gentle light.
A beacon of hope in the darkest hour,
A companion, a source of power.
    So let us cherish this metal rare,
A symbol of love beyond compare.
For silver holds the dreams we treasure,
Guiding us with its radiant measure.

THIRTY-FOUR

PASSION WITHIN

In the realm of elements, a wonder unfolds,
A metal pure, with stories untold.
Silver, oh silver, radiant and bright,
A gift from the stars, a celestial light.
    With moonlit gleam, it dances and gleams,
A shimmering symphony in silvery streams.
Its touch is gentle, its hue divine,
A solace for hearts, a grace so fine.
    Silver, oh silver, enchanting and rare,
A keeper of memories, a dreamer's affair.
It captures the fragments of time's embrace,
And weaves them into dreams, in a mystical space.
    Its aura bewitching, like moonbeams at night,
It whispers of secrets, in soft silvery light.

A guardian of dreams, it holds them so dear,
In its luminous glow, they shimmer and appear.
    Silver, oh silver, a symbol so grand,
Igniting love's flame with a delicate hand.
Its sparkle ignites the passion within,
And binds hearts together, in a love that's akin.
    So let us cherish this precious delight,
This chemical element, so pure and so bright.
For silver, oh silver, holds beauty untold,
A treasure of grace, a marvel to behold.

THIRTY-FIVE

CELESTIAL LIGHT

In the realm where dreams take flight,
There resides a guardian of the night,
Silver, the element so pure and bright,
A vessel for love and beauty's might.

Adorned in moonlight's gentle gleam,
Silver weaves a mesmerizing dream,
Reflecting stars in its shimmering stream,
A celestial dance, a silver moonbeam.

With grace and elegance, it takes its place,
A symbol of purity, an ethereal embrace,
In its radiant glow, we find solace,
A touch of silver, an angelic trace.

Silver brings peace, serenity untold,
A tranquil whisper, a story yet unfold,
Its gentle touch, like a tranquil stream,
Bringing hope and serenity to the dream.

A companion in times of joy and sorrow,
A source of strength for a brighter tomorrow,
Silver's allure, a power to borrow,
To guide us through darkness, to a brighter morrow.

And in the depths of time's intricate scheme,
Silver captures moments, like a woven dream,
Igniting passion, binding hearts together,
Its aura eternal, a love that will last forever.

So let us cherish this precious metal,
A guardian of dreams, a love vessel,
Silver, the element, so pure and bright,
A symphony of beauty, a celestial light.

ABOUT THE AUTHOR

Walter the Educator is one of the pseudonyms for Walter Anderson. Formally educated in Chemistry, Business, and Education, he is an educator, an author, a diverse entrepreneur, and he is the son of a disabled war veteran. "Walter the Educator" shares his time between educating and creating. He holds interests and owns several creative projects that entertain, enlighten, enhance, and educate, hoping to inspire and motivate you.

Follow, find new works, and stay up to date
with Walter the Educator™
at WaltertheEducator.com

www.ingramcontent.com/pod-product-compliance
Lightning Source LLC
LaVergne TN
LVHW052000060526
838201LV00059B/3744